The Breadwinner
Lit Link

Grades 4-6

Written by Nat Reed
Illustrated by Tom Goldsmith and S&S Learning Materials

About the author: Nat Reed was an elementary school teacher for 29 years. He presently teaches at Trent University in the School of Education. He is the author of the children's novel, *Thunderbird Gold* (Journey Forth Books).

ISBN 978-1-55035-865-0
Copyright 2007
All Rights Reserved * Printed in Canada

Published in the United States by:
On The Mark Press
3909 Witmer Road PMB 175
Niagara Falls, New York 14305
www.onthemarkpress.com

Published in Canada by:
S&S Learning Materials
15 Dairy Avenue
Napanee, Ontario K7R 1M4
www.sslearning.com

At A Glance

Learning Expectations	Chapter 1	Chapter 2	Chapter 3	Chapter 4	Chapter 5	Chapter 6	Chapter 7	Chapter 8	Chapter 9	Chapter 10	Chapter 11	Chapter 12	Chapter 13	Chapter 14	Chapter 15
Reading Comprehension															
• Identify and describe story elements	•	•	•	•	•	•	•	•	•	•	•	•	•	•	•
• Summarize events and details	•	•	•	•	•	•	•	•	•	•	•	•	•	•	•
Reasoning & Critical Thinking Skills															
• Identify and compare character traits	•					•	•							•	•
• Use context clues (i.e., identify analogies)				•		•	•				•			•	
• Make inferences (i.e., why events occurred, characters' thoughts and feelings, etc.)	•	•	•		•	•	•	•	•	•	•	•	•	•	•
• Determine the meaning of colloquialisms and other phrases	•	•		•								•			
• Understand abstract concepts – conscience, revenge, fear, perseverance, self-respect, exaggeration, conflict, etc.	•	•	•		•	•	•		•	•	•	•	•	•	
• Develop opinions and personal interpretations	•		•	•	•	•	•			•		•	•	•	•
• Write a letter/editorial for a newspaper						•					•				
• Conduct an interview										•					
• Develop research skills	•			•			•			•					
• Identify cliffhangers and foreshadowing	•	•			•	•						•			•
• Create a poster													•		
• Create a book cover															•
• Identify conflict							•								
• Create a time line															•
Vocabulary Development, Grammar & Word Use															
• Identify synonyms, antonyms and homonyms				•	•				•	•		•	•	•	•
• Identify similes				•											
• Identify syllables			•												
• Identify compound words												•			
• Identify descriptive words and phrases		•											•	•	•
• Identify parts of speech									•	•					
• Dictionary and thesaurus skills	•	•		•			•					•	•		•
• Place words in alphabetical order					•										
• Identify singular/plural				•											
• Identify root words											•				
• Use capitals and punctuation correctly					•										

The Breadwinner

By Deborah Ellis

Table of Contents

The Breadwinner
By Deborah Ellis

Overall Expectations

The students will:

- develop their skills in reading, writing, listening and oral communication

- use good literature as a vehicle for developing skills required by curriculum expectations: reasoning and critical thinking, knowledge of language structure, vocabulary building, and use of conventions

- become meaningfully engaged in the drama of literature through a variety of types of questions and activities

- identify and describe elements of stories (i.e. plot, main idea, characters, setting)

- learn and review many skills in order to develop good reading habits

- provide clear answers to questions and well-constructed explanations

- organize and classify information to clarify thinking

- learn about the destructive nature of the abuse of power in a society and its repercussions on the people of that society

- relate events and feelings found in novels to their own lives and experiences

- appreciate the importance of family, friendship and loyalty in personal relationships

- discern that strength is often found during difficult circumstances and is made possible through the love and support of family and friends

- learn the importance of dealing with adversity and developing perseverance in the face of adversity

- state their own interpretation of a written work, using evidence from the work and from their own knowledge and experience

The Breadwinner
By Deborah Ellis

List of Skills

Vocabulary Development

1. Identify/create similes
2. Locate descriptive words/phrases
3. List synonyms & antonyms
4. Use capitals and punctuation correctly
5. Identify syllables
6. List compound words
7. Use singular/plural nouns correctly
8. Use context clues (analogies)
9. Identify parts of speech
10. Determine alphabetical order
11. Determine meaning of Dari words
12. Identify of root words

Setting Activities

1. Summarize the details of a setting
2. Identify hardships of living in oppressive society
3. Create a time chart

Plot Activities

1. Complete a time line of events
2. Identify foreshadowing
3. Determine the role of others in one's personal growth
4. Identify conflict in the story
5. Identify cliffhangers

Character Activities

1. Determine character traits
2. Compare two characters
3. Understand concepts such as perseverance, self respect, stereotypes, tolerance
4. Relate personal experiences

Creative and Critical Thinking

1. Research the country of Afghanistan
2. Write an editorial on an issue
3. Write a description of personal feelings
4. Conduct an interview
5. Write a letter to a friend

Art Activities

1. Design a poster
2. Design a cover for the novel

The Breadwinner
By Deborah Ellis

Teacher Suggestions

This resource can be used in a variety of ways:

1. The student booklet focuses on one chapter of the novel at a time. Each of these sections contains the following activities:
   a) **Before you read the chapter** (reasoning and critical thinking skills)
   b) **Vocabulary building** (dictionary and thesaurus skills)
   c) **Questions on the chapter** (reading comprehension skills)
   d) **Language activities** (grammar, punctuation, word structure & usage, writing)
   e) **Extension activities** (research, social studies, art & other modes of communication)

2. Students may read the novel at their own speed and then select, or be assigned, a variety of questions and activities.

3. **Bulletin Board and Interest Center Ideas:** themes might include: Afghanistan (people, culture, religion, agricultural products, geography, historical characters); or heroic women

4. **Pre-Reading Activities:** *The Breadwinner* may also be used in conjunction with themes of self-esteem, perseverance, family values, societal prejudice (the role of women), the danger of stereotyping, and the difficulties experienced when a young person is forced to take on too many responsibilities in a family.

5. **Independent Reading Approach:** Students who are able to work independently may attempt to complete the assignments in a self-directed manner. Initially these students should participate in the pre-reading activities with the rest of the class. Students should familiarize themselves with the reproducible student booklet. Completed worksheets should be submitted so that the teacher can note how quickly and accurately the students are working. Students may be brought together periodically to discuss issues in specific sections of the novel.

6. **Fine Art Activities:** students may integrate such topics as Afghanistan, farm crops of the middle east, modes of transportation in this region, beadwork and other small crafts.

7. Encourage the students to keep a reading log in which they record their readings each day and their thoughts about the passage.

8. Students should keep all their work together in one place. A portfolio cover is provided for this reason.

9. Students should not be expected to complete all activities. Teachers should allow choice and in some cases match the activity to the student's ability.

10. Students should keep track (in their portfolio) of the activities they complete.

The Breadwinner

By Deborah Ellis

Synopsis

The Breadwinner is the engaging story of an eleven year Afghani girl named Parvana. Set in the country of Afghanistan during the rule of the Taliban, Parvana and her family have rarely been outdoors for a year and a half. No longer can she or her siblings attend school, or even play outdoors. Despite her parents' university education and enlightened views, they are all trapped within the four walls of a tiny one room apartment. The family's situation becomes perilous when Parvana's father is taken away to jail by the Taliban. It is then that Parvana is forced to take on the responsibility of being the "breadwinner" for her small family. Disguised as a boy, Parvana goes out to the marketplace each day to offer her skills as a reader. Here Parvana realizes a freedom that she has not known since the Taliban came to power. She and her friend, Shauzia, later become "tea boys" and finally earn money digging up bones in a local cemetery. Parvana is a very appealing character who will strike a chord with most North American readers. The author's portrayal of Parvana and her family through their heartache and trials is both realistic and thought-provoking.

The Breadwinner is an engrossing novel that delves into the harsh realities of life for girls and women in modern-day Afghanistan. Ellis based her novel on the true-life stories of women in Afghan refugee camps.

Author Biography

Deborah Ellis

Deborah Ellis was born in the small northern Ontario town of Cochrane and grew up in Moosonee and Paris, Ontario, where she attended school. As a young girl Deborah enjoyed biking and reading more than she did being a student. By the time she was 12 years old she had already decided to become a writer.

In secondary school Deborah volunteered in the Peace Movement and honed her writing skills by entering a number of writing contests. Anti-war themes became the focus for much of Deborah's writing after she graduated. She traveled to countries such as Afghanistan, Russia and Israel to research her novels and learn more of the people in these countries.

In 2000 she won the Governor General's Award for her first novel, *Looking for X*. Her 1997 trip to Afghanistan led to the writing of her renowned trio of books: *The Breadwinner*, *Parvana's Journey*, and *Mud City* as well as the adult book *Women of the Afghan War*. *The Breadwinner* was actually inspired by an interview with an Afghan mother in a refugee camp.

All the royalties from Deborah's books go to charities, such as *Women for Women in Afghanistan*, UNICEF and *Street Kids International*. She continues to travel the world, giving a voice to people who often have interesting, but tragic, stories that desperately need to be told.

The Breadwinner

By Deborah Ellis

Student Checklist

Student Name: _____

Assignment	Grade/Level	Comments

The Breadwinner
By Deborah Ellis

Name: _____

The Breadwinner
By Deborah Ellis

Chapter 1

Before you read the chapter:

The Breadwinner is set in the country of Afghanistan. Do you know this about Afghanistan? Although its population (30 million) is almost the same as Canada's, Canada is 15 times larger. Most Afghanis are Sunni and Shiite Muslim. The average life expectancy of an Afghani is 46 years. Natural gas, dried fruits and nuts, carpets, leather and crafts are the country's main exports. Now do some investigating of your own and come up with at least three additional interesting facts about this country and its people.

_____

_____

_____

What does the term "breadwinner" mean? From the title and the picture on the novel's cover, predict why this might be an appropriate title for this novel.

_____

_____

Vocabulary:

1. Many of the words that you will encounter in this novel are words unfamiliar to most North Americans, but familiar to the people of Afghanistan. Using the Glossary at the back of the novel or other sources, match each word with its meaning.

   a) chador

   b) Taliban

   c) dari

   d) burqa

   e) Kabul

   1. a long, tent-like garment worn by women

   2. cloth worn by women and girls to cover their hair and shoulders

   3. the capital city of Afghanistan

   4. members of a political party in Afghanistan

   5. one of two main languages spoken in Afghanistan

The Breadwinner

By Deborah Ellis

2. Choose a word from the list to complete each sentence.

collapse	decreed	respected	labyrinth	definite
urn	hawked	peddler	militia	disrupt

a) The soldiers decided to _____ the meeting.

b) During the hard times in our country, my mother _____ her jewelry.

c) Parvana bought a grapefruit from an old _____ in the marketplace.

d) The potter made a beautiful _____ which he gave to my sister for a wedding gift.

e) The streets of Kabul were like a _____ to most newcomers.

f) The _____ seized control of the country when the king died.

g) My teacher was very _____ about my answer being wrong.

h) No one expected the building to _____.

i) The Taliban _____ that all women and girls must remain indoors at all times.

j) Parvana's parents were once _____ members of the community.

3. Put the following expressions from this chapter in your own words:

Holding her tongue: _____

_____

Afghans cover the earth like stars cover the sky: _____

_____

The sound of the family's laughter scampered up Mount Parvana:

_____

_____

The Breadwinner
By Deborah Ellis

Questions:

1. Name two of the restrictions that the Taliban had placed upon the girls and women of Afghanistan.

   _____

   _____

2. How would you describe Parvana? You may consider facts about her appearance or personality.

   _____

   _____

3. a) How did Parvana's father now earn a living?

   _____

   b) How had he once earned his living?

   _____

4. The Taliban militia had some very definite ideas about how things should be run in Afghanistan. Identify one of these ideas that you found particularly upsetting.

   _____

   _____

5. Describe the responsibilities of the "tea boys".

   _____

   _____

6. Describe why it would be difficult for a family to live in one room together.

   _____

   _____

7. The author states, "Each time, they moved to a smaller place." Explain why this happened to Parvana's family.

   _____

   _____

The Breadwinner
By Deborah Ellis

8. **a)** How did Nooria explain to Parvana why the Soviets left Afghanistan?

_____

b) What does this tell you about Nooria's personality?

_____

Language Activities:

1. With a straight line, match each character from _The Breadwinner_ with a description of that character.

   a) Parvana   Five years old

   b) Maryam   The oldest sister

   c) Ali   Was in grade six

   d) Nooria   Two years old

2. **Foreshadowing** is defined as **to suggest beforehand** (or to hint as to what is about to happen). The author of _The Breadwinner_ provides the reader with a hint of what may happen in the story with the mention of the "tea boys" and their responsibilities. How might this prove to be an example of foreshadowing?

_____
_____
_____
_____
_____
_____
_____
_____
_____

The Breadwinner
By Deborah Ellis

Chapter 2

Before you read the chapter:

What are some of the freedoms you are able to enjoy in the country in which you live?

_____

_____

_____

_____

What things are in place in your country that helps to protect these freedoms?

_____

_____

_____

_____

Vocabulary:

1. Many of the words that you will encounter in this novel are unfamiliar to most North Americans, but familiar to the people of Afghanistan. Using the Glossary at the back of the novel or other sources, find the meaning of each of the words on the left.

toshak	
shalwar kameez	
Eid	
Nan	
turban	

The Breadwinner

By Deborah Ellis

2. Using words from this chapter, complete the following crossword puzzle.

Nooria	looters	vibrant	Malali	stove	tent	smart
Parvana	imitate	noon	drag	ate	one	silk
resentful	dangerous	embroidery	relent	shut	treat	propane
intricate	rouse	illiterate	foreign			

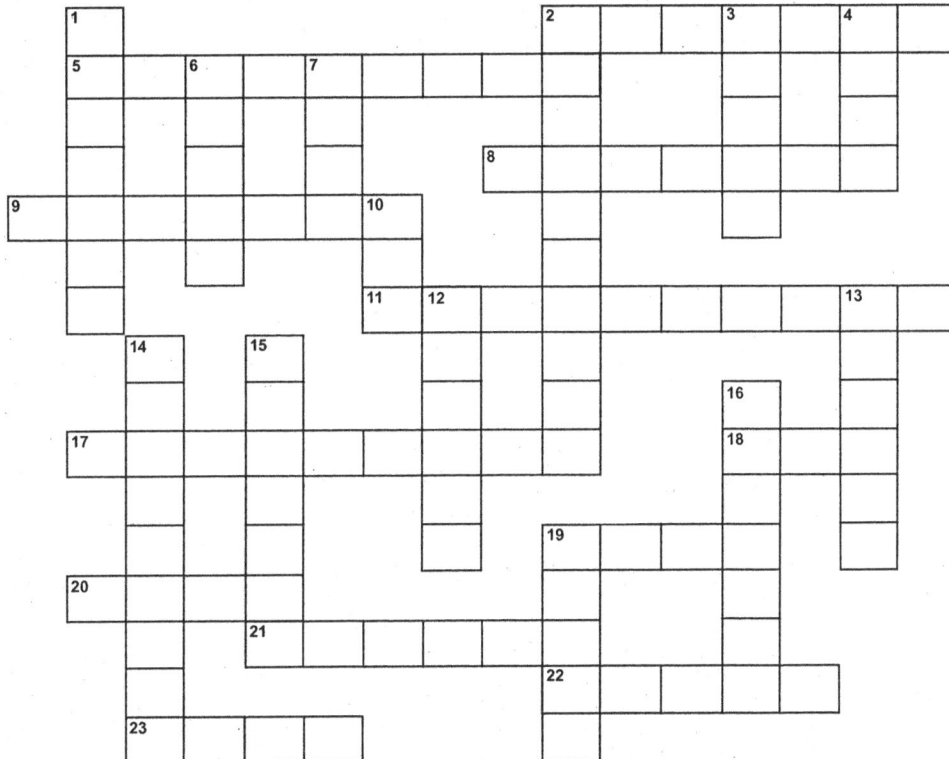

Across

2. To copy
5. Dissatisfied
8. Lively
9. The novel's main character
11. Decorative needlework
17. Complicated
18. A number less than two
19. Not open
20. To pull along or haul
21. Parvana's older sister
22. To wake up
23. A rich type of material

Down

1. A type of gas
2. Unable to read and write
3. Trick or _____
4. A canvas dwelling
6. An instrument used for heat and/or cooking
7. Middle of the day
10. Consumed
12. An Afghan heroine
13. To give in
14. Perilous
15. Alien
16. Robbers
19. Clever

The Breadwinner

By Deborah Ellis

Questions:

1. Why was it dangerous for a woman to go outside without a man in Kabul (the city where Parvana lived)?

   _____

   _____

2. Why do you think Parvana's mother and sister cleaned the cupboard so often?

   _____

   _____

3. Father mentions that the Taliban encouraged neighbors to spy on neighbors. What information might the Taliban be interested in having reported to them?

   _____

   _____

4. Why did Parvan's mother refuse to sell Nooria's good clothes?

   _____

   _____

5. Explain the statement, "she'd (Parvana) hate her mother, too, if she wasn't her mother".

   _____

   _____

6. What had happened to Parvana's older brother, Hossain?

   _____

   _____

7. What did it mean that Parvana's family ate "Afghan-style"?

   _____

   _____

8. In the story told by Parvana's father, describe how Malali inspired the Afghan soldiers?

   _____

   _____

The Breadwinner
By Deborah Ellis

9. What do you think Parvana's father meant by the statement, "there are many types of battles"?

_____

_____

10. Why did the soldiers invade Parvana's home?

_____

_____

Language Activities:

The author really leaves the reader wondering what will happen to Parvana and her family. This is a literary device called a **cliffhanger**.

Predict what you think might happen to Parvana's family. Consider the fate of her father, and what might happen to the family if he does not return.

_____

_____

_____

_____

_____

_____

_____

_____

_____

_____

_____

_____

The Breadwinner
By Deborah Ellis

Chapter 3

Before you read the chapter:

Losing your home and most of your possessions would probably be one of the worst things that could ever happen. What are a few important **personal possessions** a person might lose if his or her home was taken away?

_____

_____

_____

Vocabulary:

In each of the following sets of words, circle the one word that does not belong. Then write a sentence explaining why it does not fit.

1. protest   agree   dissent   resist

_____

2. celebration   regulation   law   ordinance

_____

3. lavatory   bathroom   privy   laboratory

_____

4. distinguish   tell apart   devotion   discern

_____

5. affluent   committed   performed   perpetrated

_____

6. pranced   hobbled   stumbled   staggered

_____

7. militia   army   military   drillers

_____

The Breadwinner

By Deborah Ellis

Questions:

Complete the following exercise filling in the correct words from the list.

apartment	floor	guards	snoring	prison	women
Parvana	father	burqa	photograph	Malali	beat

After waking up following her father's arrest, Parvana and her family decided to clean up their _____. The family slept on quilts and blankets spread over the _____. In the past, whenever Parvana awoke in the night, the sound of her father's _____ made her think that everything was alright.

Parvana's mother had often said, "You can't be truly Afghan if you don't know someone who's been in _____." The Talaban had ordered that all windows be painted black so that no one could see the _____ inside.

Parvana's mother decided that she and _____ would get her husband out of jail. Nooria wrote her a note which pretended to be from their _____ giving Parvana's mother permission to be outside by herself. The billowing _____ Parvana's mother was wearing made it hard for her to see where she was going. Along the way they used a _____ to ask people if they had seen Parvana's father. At the prison Parvana and her mother told the _____ that they wanted to see Parvana's father. To give her strength, Parvana imagined she was the Afghan heroine, _____. Parvana and her mother finally gave up and left the prison after the guards began to _____ them.

The Breadwinner

By Deborah Ellis

Language Activities:

1. This chapter contains several statements that show how grim it must have been to live in Afghanistan at this time:

   - "You can't be truly Afghan if you don't know someone who's been in prison."
   - "Buses were not permitted to carry women who did not have a man with them."
   - "Photographs were illegal."
   - "Any one of these people could turn Parvana and her mother into the militia."

   From these sentences and others that you have read in the novel, describe how you would feel if you were living in Afghanistan at this time.

   _____

   _____

   _____

   _____

   How might you have protected yourself from the Taliban and being thrown in prison?

   _____

   _____

   _____

2. Choose 10 words from this chapter with two or more **syllables**. Indicate the syllables by drawing a line between each syllable. **Example:** wa/ter.

   _____   _____

   _____   _____

   _____   _____

   _____   _____

   _____   _____

The Breadwinner

By Deborah Ellis

Chapter 4

Before you read the chapter:

Tell what you think the following statements mean, and give your impression of each of them:

- The two foes of human happiness are pain and boredom. (Arthur Schopenhauer)

_____

_____

_____

- There's no excuse to be bored. (Viggo Mortensen)

_____

_____

_____

Vocabulary:

Draw a straight line to connect the vocabulary word to its definition. Remember to use a straight edge (like a ruler). Be careful – a few are very similar in meaning!

1. exhaustion	a)	heed
2. collapse	b)	extreme fright
3. preoccupied	c)	staying alive
4. concentration	d)	engrossment
5. survive	e)	suitable
6. waddle	f)	think about
7. attention	g)	break down
8. decent	h)	obsessed
9. consider	i)	extreme tiredness
10. terrified	j)	totter

The Breadwinner

By Deborah Ellis

Questions:

1. How long had it been since Parvana's mother had been out of the house?
   _____

2. a) What reason did Parvana's mother give for not continuing her writing?
   _____

   b) Why did her husband think it was important for her to continue to write?
   _____

3. a) Why wouldn't Parvana's father leave Afghanistan?
   _____
   _____

   b) Do you think this was a wise decision? Explain.
   _____
   _____

4. Why were there no secrets in their family?
   _____

5. a) What do you think Parvana meant by saying, "Everybody leans on everybody in this family"?
   _____
   _____

   b) When Nooria responded to Parvana's observation with the words, "And who do I lean on?" What does the author mean when she says that it was "such a Nooria-like comment"?
   _____
   _____

6. Why did Parvana think it was her mother's responsibility to get food for the family when they ran out?
   _____
   _____

The Breadwinner

By Deborah Ellis

7. **a)** What would a doctor probably say was wrong with Parvana's mother at the end of the chapter?

   _____

   _____

   b) What caused this condition?

   _____

   _____

8. Why do you think Parvana decided to obey her sister and go out to buy food?

   _____

   _____

Language Activities:

1. A **simile** is a type of literary device that makes a comparison using the words "like" or "as". "Her father's face was like a jigsaw puzzle" is an example of a simile from this chapter. This simile compares Parvana's father's face with a jigsaw puzzle. Create your own similes in the following comparisons:

   a) the beauty of a person with a specific type of flower

   _____

   b) the age of a person with _____ (your choice)

   _____

   c) a simile comparing two things of your choice

   _____

The Breadwinner
By Deborah Ellis

2. Write the plural of the following nouns from this chapter. Careful – you may wish to consult a dictionary for some of these words.

Singular Noun	Plural Noun
sandal	
burqa	
foot	
family	
wife	
parent	
country	
tongue	
piece	
person	

Extension activities:

The author paints a vivid picture of life in Afghanistan under the Taliban. You already know quite a bit about this fascinating country and its people, but there is probably a lot that you are also curious about. Your task is to do some investigative research on Afghanistan and its people. Before you begin your research, list details in the first two columns. Fill in the last column after completing the research. Try to come up with at least three items for each column. Use another sheet of paper if you run out of room.

Topic:		
What I Know	**What I Want to Know**	**What I Learned**

The Breadwinner
By Deborah Ellis

Chapter 5

Before you read the chapter:

Describe a time in your life when you were treated disrespectfully. What happened? How did it make you feel? Why do you think this incident caused you to feel this way?

_____

_____

_____

_____

_____

Vocabulary:

Choose a word from the list that means the same or nearly the same as the underlined word(s).

fetch	obedient	an eternity	consider	selections
warily	anxious	circumstance	sensible	attendant

1. Caleb always found it hard to make good **choices**.   _____

2. The rich man's **servant** was most helpful.   _____

3. It's hard not to be **worried** during stressful times.   _____

4. It was a very funny **situation**.   _____

5. Running away from the lion was the **sane** thing to do.   _____

6. You must back away from an angry dog **carefully**.   _____

7. Go and **get** me my morning newspaper.   _____

8. It seemed like **forever** before her mother awoke.   _____

9. Please **think about** choosing me for your partner.   _____

10. He was very **compliant** when he was around the Taliban.   _____

The Breadwinner
By Deborah Ellis

Questions:

1. Why were shopkeepers sometimes beaten for serving women inside their shops?

   _____

2. Why was Parvana sent out into the marketplace? Why was she the one chosen to go instead of another family member?

   _____

   _____

3. Describe what happened in the market that frightened Parvana.

   _____

   _____

4. From what we know about Mrs. Weera in this chapter, how would you describe her personality?

   _____

   _____

5. How was Mrs. Weera good for Parvana's family? Why do you think this was so?

   _____

   _____

6. Why do you think Nooria was especially glad to see Mrs. Weera?

   _____

   _____

7. Why was it necessary to boil the water?

   _____

   _____

8. Once again the author leaves us with a **cliffhanger** at the end of Chapter Five. Predict what might happen based on the last statement in this chapter, "I guess we'll have to think of something else".

   _____

   _____

The Breadwinner

By Deborah Ellis

9. Why do you think Mrs. Weera's presence had such a good effect on Parvana's mother?

_____

_____

Language Activities:

1. Despite the dangers, at one point in this chapter Parvana almost drinks the unboiled water because she is so thirsty. Such a decision is often called **rash**. Can you think of a personal experience when you make a rash decision similar to the one Parvana almost made? Perhaps, like Parvana, you had second thoughts before actually committing yourself to a dangerous choice. Tell about the incident, and the decision you made.

_____

_____

_____

_____

_____

2. Place the following words from this chapter in **alphabetical order**.

shopkeepers	1. _____
servants	2. _____
smell	3. _____
swallowed	4. _____
selection	5. _____
stick	6. _____
magazine	7. _____
shoulder	8. _____
squeezing	9. _____
suddenly	10. _____

The Breadwinner
By Deborah Ellis

Chapter 6

Before you read the chapter:

In *The Breadwinner*, members of Parvana's family resort to telling a number of lies in order to survive. Considering the circumstances described in the novel, do you think it was right for Parvana's family to tell lies? Defend your answer.

_____

_____

_____

Vocabulary:

Solve the following word search puzzle using the words from the box. Remember – the words can be horizontal, vertical or diagonal. They may be forward or even backward!

adjustment	idle	decision	sulk	brusquely
gingerly	recognize	pakul	chador	fumed
fake	invisible	hesitate	ordinary	toshak
complimented	Hossain	Parvana	Nooria	solution

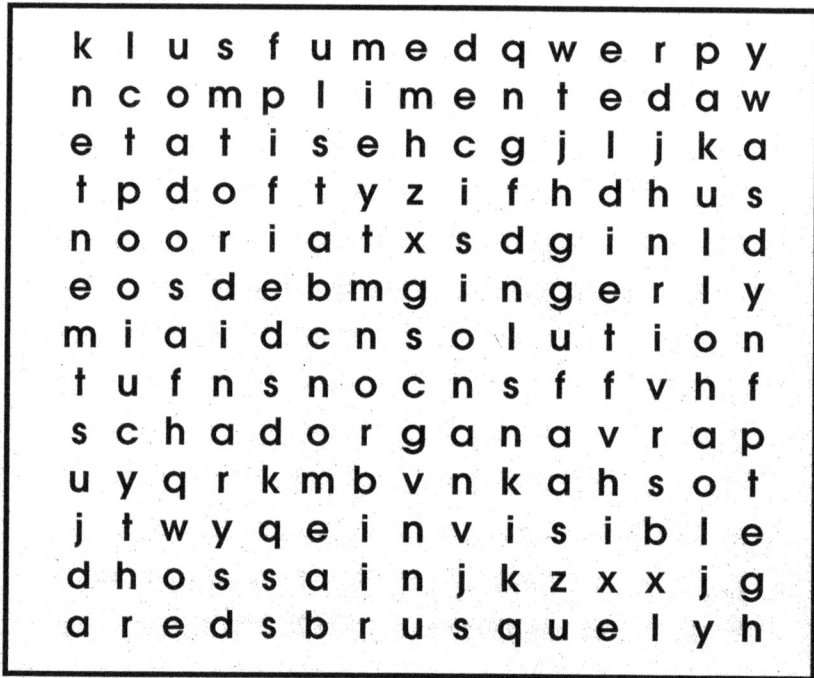

```
k l u s f u m e d q w e r p y
n c o m p l i m e n t e d a w
e t a t i s e h c g j l j k a
t p d o f t y z i f h d h u s
n o o r i a t x s d g i n l d
e o s d e b m g i n g e r l y
m i a i d c n s o l u t i o n
t u f n s n o c n s f f v h f
s c h a d o r g a n a v r a p
u y q r k m b v n k a h s o t
j t w y q e i n v i s i b l e
d h o s s a i n j k z x x j g
a r e d s b r u s q u e l y h
```

The Breadwinner

By Deborah Ellis

Questions:

1. What was your first thought when you read the introductory statement: "They were going to turn her into a boy"?

   _____

   _____

2. Why would there be no one to question the sudden "disappearance" of Parvana and the appearance of her "cousin"?

   _____

3. Why was this transformation especially hard on:

   Parvana?_____

   Her mother? _____

4. Why do think Parvana told her mother to throw away the hair that had been cut off?

   _____

5. Why was Parvana so terrified about going out into the marketplace dressed as a boy? What might be the consequences of her being caught?

   _____

   _____

6. Why was it a good idea that Parvana continue to dress as a boy while she was inside the house?

   _____

7. Why do you think Nooria treated Parvana so poorly most of the time?

   _____

   _____

8. a) What do you make of the last paragraph in this chapter?

   _____

   b) Why do you think Parvana's mother said this?

   _____

The Breadwinner
By Deborah Ellis

Language Activities:

1. Rewrite the following sentences putting in the **correct capitalization and punctuation**.

   parvana's brother, hossain, was killed by a land mine

   _____

   _____

   the afghan city of kabul was seriously damaged by years of war

   _____

   _____

   what kind of president would it take to restore order in afghanistan

   _____

   _____

2. Much has happened to Parvana already in this novel. With a partner **make a list** of the most important adventures that Parvana and her family have endured during this short time. Then using this list, pretend that you are Parvana and **write a letter on a separate piece of paper** to her friend, Marisol, who now lives in Pakistan. Be sure to tell Marisol about the exiting things that have happened to you and describe your feelings throughout this time.

   List Parvana and her family's adventures:

The Breadwinner

By Deborah Ellis

Chapter 7

Before you read the chapter:

It is often difficult to understand the point of view of someone you don't particularly like, especially if they treat you badly. Why do you think Nooria was often cruel to her younger sister, Parvana? Do you think the unkind things she said to Parvana was an accurate reflection of her personality? Give reasons for your answer.

_____

_____

_____

_____

Vocabulary:

Write a **sentence** using the following words. Make sure that the meaning of the word is clear in your sentence.

disguise: _____

_____

vendor: _____

_____

labyrinth: _____

_____

hesitated: _____

_____

regret: _____

_____

Questions:

1. What motivated Parvana to go back outside dressed as a boy?

_____

The Breadwinner

By Deborah Ellis

2. What was the advantage to always returning to the same place in the market each and every day?

   _____

3. Consider the following sentence from this chapter: "She was certain that at any moment someone would stop, point at her and yell, 'Girl'. The word would ring out through the market like a curse". What does this statement tell you about Parvana's situation at this time.

   _____

   _____

4. What did the Talib ask Parvana to do for him?

   _____

5. From the letter, list two things we learn about the following two people:

   the niece: _____

   _____

   the aunt: _____

   _____

6. What did you learn about this member of the Taliban from this incident?

   _____

   _____

7. What would be a possible advantage and disadvantage to Parvana's strategy of letting the customer pay **whatever they liked** for the reading of a letter?

   Advantage: _____

   _____

   Disadvantage: _____

   _____

The Breadwinner
By Deborah Ellis

8. What would be an advantage and a disadvantage to the **bartering** system also described in this chapter?

Advantage: _____

_____

Disadvantage: _____

_____

Language Activities:

1. The second last paragraph in Chapter 7 might be an example of **foreshadowing** (a literary device in which the author drops hints about what might come later in the story). Reread this paragraph and predict what might develop from this brief incident.

_____

_____

_____

_____

2. **Conflict** is an important element in a novel. There are generally three types of conflict: **person against person**; **person against self**; and **person against nature**. Find three examples of conflict in *The Breadwinner*, and tell which type of conflict each is.

a) Type of Conflict: _____

_____

_____

_____

b) Type of Conflict: _____

_____

_____

_____

The Breadwinner
By Deborah Ellis

c) Type of Conflict:_____

_____

_____

_____

Extension Activities:

Very little is said in this novel of the foods that the typical Afghani eats other than the occasional reference to such foods as **nan** and **kebab**. Investigate other foods that a person from Afghanistan might eat during better times than those described in this novel. Try to come up with at least three Afghan foods and a description of each.

_____

_____

_____

_____

_____

_____

_____

_____

_____

The Breadwinner
By Deborah Ellis

Chapter 8

Before you read the chapter:

Describe what you think would be most difficult about being stuck inside one small room with all of your family members for a year and a half.

_____

_____

_____

Vocabulary:

Choose a word from the list to complete each definition.

relent	escort	distinctive	athletics	routine
dawdling	splendid	pneumonia	collided	position

1. Something that is run of the mill is said to be _____.

2. A _____ is somewhere where something is located.

3. When someone is taking their time, they may be _____ .

4. Bugs Bunny has a very _____ voice.

5. _____ is a serious lung infection.

6. Something which is very beautiful can be said to be _____.

7. A person who is physically fit may also be good at _____.

8. To _____ can mean to change one's mind.

9. If you accompany someone to a party or dance, you are that person's _____.

10. When two automobiles run into each other head-on, they have _____.

The Breadwinner
By Deborah Ellis

Questions:

Indicate whether the following statements are **true** or **false**.

1. Mrs. Weera and Parvana's mother decided to produce a television news special. T or F

2. Mrs. Weera had once been a schoolteacher. T or F

3. Bombs, the war, and pneumonia killed most of the Weeras. T or F

4. Mrs. Weera was once the fastest swimmer in Afghanistan. T or F

5. When Parvana is outside she is called Hussein. T or F

6. Maryam had to wear an old pair of Nooria's sandals when she went outside with Parvana. T or F

7. The water at the tap had to be boiled before drinking. T or F

8. Parvana had to come home from the market each day at noon to use the latrine. T or F

9. Parvana's mother was able to take the small children outside for several hours each day. T or F

10. One day Parvana saw her father walking in the marketplace. T or F

Language Activities:

Choose any two characters you've already met in this novel. Compare four things about these two people. Consider such things as physical appearance, personality, age, talents, attitude, etc.

	Character 1 _____	Character 2 _____
1		
2		
3		
4		

The Breadwinner

By Deborah Ellis

Chapter 9

Before you read the chapter:

If it was possible for a girl to receive an education in Afghanistan during this time, how might this be an advantage? How might it not be very useful?

_____

_____

_____

Vocabulary:

Synonyms are words with similar meanings. Using the context of the sentences below, choose the best synonym for the underlined words in each sentence.

1. My little brother never **complains**, no matter what the circumstances.
   - **a)** grumbles
   - **b)** compliments
   - **c)** compares
   - **d)** inhabits

2. The angry driver's **gestures** were very rude.
   - **a)** thoughts
   - **b)** cursing
   - **c)** motions
   - **d)** recordings

3. Overjoyed, Shauzia **embraced** Parvana when they first met.
   - **a)** hugged
   - **b)** kissed
   - **c)** shook hands
   - **d)** wept

4. They had to **smuggle** the item past customs.
   - **a)** export
   - **b)** sneak
   - **c)** bribe
   - **d)** wrestle

5. My little sister looked **ridiculous** in Uncle John's hockey equipment.
   - **a)** somber
   - **b)** humorous
   - **c)** sordid
   - **d)** absurd

6. The editor decided to **publish** the manuscript.
   - **a)** obliterate
   - **b)** discard
   - **c)** print
   - **d)** circumscript

7. They had to go to the marketplace to purchase more **kerosene**.
   - **a)** fuel
   - **b)** margarine
   - **c)** chilblains
   - **d)** light bulbs

8. **Apricots** were quite expensive in Kabul during this time.
   - **a)** vegetables
   - **b)** fruit
   - **c)** beans
   - **d)** dried onions

The Breadwinner

By Deborah Ellis

Questions:

1. Chapter 8 leaves the reader in suspense. Who was the unexpected person that Parvana met, and what was she doing in the marketplace?

   _____

   _____

2. What special treat did Parvana receive from her new friend?

   _____

3. What happened to Shauzia's brother and father? Why would this be especially difficult for the rest of the family?

   _____

   _____

4. According to Shauzia, what happened to most people who were sent to prison by the Taliban?

   _____

5. Shauzia suggested that perhaps she and Parvana might come up with a better way to make money. Can you think of any ideas that might be possibilities in this regard?

   _____

   _____

6. Why did Shauzia insist that Parvana back her up when Parvana's mother tried to get her to stay for tea?

   _____

   _____

7. Why would selling things off a tray be an advantage considering what the girls were already doing?

   _____

   _____

8. What two projects was Mrs. Weera thinking of starting?

   _____

   _____

The Breadwinner
By Deborah Ellis

9. Why was Nooria excited?

_____

10. Who was the window woman, and what was she doing that caught Parvana's attention?

_____

_____

11. Once again another chapter ends in a cliffhanger. What possible job could Shauzia have in mind that Parvana didn't like? Try to think of at least two possibilities.

_____

_____

Language Activities:

1. Copy out any three sentences from this chapter and underline the **verbs**.

_____

_____

_____

_____

_____

_____

_____

_____

_____

2. Beside each of the following words from this chapter, write its **root word**.

watching _____   dressed _____

carefully _____   bossier _____

excitement _____   sweetness _____

heard _____   invited _____

The Breadwinner
By Deborah Ellis

Extension Activities:

Create a **book cover** for *The Breadwinner*. Be sure to include the title, author, and a picture that will make other students want to read the novel.

The Breadwinner

By Deborah Ellis

Chapter 10

Before you read the chapter:

What has been the most unpleasant job you have ever had to do? What made this particular task so unpleasant?

_____

_____

_____

Vocabulary:

Antonyms are words with opposite meanings. Draw a line from each word in Column A to its antonym in Column B. Then use the words in Column A to fill in the blanks in the sentences below.

Column A	Column B
obedient	apart
intact	forget
stingy	defiant
accommodate	turn away
recognize	generous

1. The hotel manager tried to _____ as many travelers as she could.

2. The item in the parcel remained _____ after its delivery.

3. I did not _____ your sister after her grave illness.

4. The puppy was trained very quickly to be _____ to its owner.

5. The old miser was most _____ with his money.

The Breadwinner
By Deborah Ellis

Questions:

1. **a)** What was the new job that Shauzia had found for herself and Parvana?

   _____

   b) Describe your own personal feelings about doing such a job?

   _____

   _____

2. What did the bone broker do with the collected bones?

   _____

3. What did the girls find to act as their mascot?

   _____

4. Just after the girls had filled the blanket with bones, Parvana was faced with a dilemma. What was it?

   _____

   _____

5. **a)** Why were some of the land mines designed as toys?

   _____

   b) What are your thoughts on this?

   _____

   _____

6. How long would it have taken Parvana to earn as much as they did that day with her job in the marketplace?

   _____

   _____

7. **a)** Why did the girls decide to hold some of the money back from their families?

   _____

   _____

   b) Was this a wise decision? Defend your answer.

   _____

   _____

The Breadwinner
By Deborah Ellis

8. Other than to clean her face, why did Parvana stick her whole head under the water tap?

_____

_____

Language Activities:

1. Find three examples of the following parts of speech from this chapter.

Nouns	Verbs	Adjectives
_____	_____	_____
_____	_____	_____
_____	_____	_____

2. **Interview** at least three other students for their views of this novel so far in their reading. (Try to get both positive and negative comments.) Write a brief **report** on a separate sheet of paper putting these views together.

1. _____

_____

_____

2. _____

_____

_____

3. _____

_____

_____

The Breadwinner

By Deborah Ellis

Chapter 11

Before you read the chapter:

Parvana's mother makes the following statement in Chapter 11: "So this is what we've become in Afghanistan. We dig up the bones of our ancestors in order to feed our families." Why do you think Parvana's actions seem to be more horrifying to her mother than Parvana herself?

_____

_____

_____

Vocabulary:

Analogies are equations in which the first pair of words has the same relationship as the second pair of words. For example, **stop** is to **go** as **fast** is to **slow**. In this example, both pairs of words are opposites. Choose the best word from the list to complete each of the analogies below.

relent	disrespect	firmly	intimidate	ordinary
terrified	declared	stint	escort	calm

1. **Long** is to **short** as **loosely** is to _____.

2. **Graceful** is to **elegant** as **placid** is to _____.

3. **Wonderful** is to **fantastic** as **scared** is to _____.

4. **Sensitive** is to **tender** as **stated** is to _____.

5. **Thick** is to **thin** as **resist** is to _____.

6. **Esteem** is to _____ as **love** is to **hate**.

7. **Rare** is to _____ as **proud** is to **humble**.

8. **Threaten** is to _____ as **stay** is to **remain**.

The Breadwinner
By Deborah Ellis

9. **Accompany** is to _____ as **graveyard** is to **cemetery**.

10. **Task** is to _____ as **stadium** is to **arena**.

Questions:

1. Why do you think Parvana decided to tell her mother the truth about her new job?

   _____

   _____

2. What were the bones used for?

   _____

   _____

3. What was especially unusual about Parvana telling her mother "no", when her mother said that she could no longer dig for bones?

   _____

   _____

4. Do you agree with Mrs. Weera's statement, "I suppose human beings are also animals"? Why do you think she said this?

   _____

   _____

5. **a)** Explain what Mrs. Weera meant by saying, "These are unusual times. They call for ordinary people to do unusual things, just to get by."

   _____

   _____

   b) What are your thoughts about Mrs. Weera's statement? Are there limits to this viewpoint?

   _____

   _____

6. When Parvana and Shauzia were deciding what to include on their trays to sell, what was one of the criteria that they established in helping them to decide?

   _____

The Breadwinner
By Deborah Ellis

7. Why do you think Nooria changed for the better in her treatment of Parvana during this time?

_____

_____

8. Describe briefly the horrifying scene that the girls witnessed in the stadium.

_____

_____

_____

Language Activities:

1. Imagine you are helping Parvana's mother work on the magazine they will be distributing to the people of Afghanistan and to interested people around the world. Write a brief **editorial** describing the events that Parvana witnessed in the stadium in this chapter. Write the editorial not only describing the events that happened, but also stating your opinion about what transpired and the way you feel about it.

_____

_____

_____

_____

_____

_____

_____

_____

_____

_____

_____

_____

_____

_____

_____

_____

The Breadwinner
By Deborah Ellis

Chapter 12

Before you read the chapter:

Like many of the people of Afghanistan during this time, Shauzia desperately wants to escape her home life and the horrors of her war-torn country. What important factors do you think she needs to consider before acting on this wish? Try to consider as many critical details as possible. (e.g., You should think about not only how the move will affect her but her family as well.)

_____

_____

_____

_____

_____

Vocabulary:

Replace the words that are underlined in the sentences below with a word from the list. Remember to consider the context of the word in the sentences, as some words have several meanings.

snippet	fertile	tempted	depend	ceased
preferred	enthusiastic	nomads	incident	insisted

1. Parvana wasn't at all **eager** to begin digging up bones. _____

2. Nooria **wanted** to stay with her mother. _____

3. You can't **rely** on an untrustworthy person. _____

4. Some Afghanis are **wanderers**. _____

5. He **stipulated** that she would have to work for him. _____

6. The farmland was very **productive**. _____

7. Only a **scrap** of the carpet remained after the explosion. _____

The Breadwinner
By Deborah Ellis

8. She **stopped** believing in Santa Claus when she was four. _____

9. The **event** was documented in all the newspapers. _____

10. The actress was **lured** by the promise of riches and fame. _____

Questions:

1. Why did Parvana need a break and want to stay home for awhile?

   _____

   _____

2. Why do you think the Taliban hated music?

   _____

   _____

3. **a)** Why did the idea of going to France appeal to Shauzia?

   _____

   _____

   b) What difficulties would she have to overcome to achieve this dream?

   _____

   _____

4. Analyze the details of Shauzia's plan to escape to France. Is it realistic? Explain your answer.

   _____

   _____

5. Who did the girls imagine the mystery woman in the window to be?

   _____

6. How might Parvana and Shauzia have taken advantage of the mystery woman's talents?

   _____

   _____

The Breadwinner

By Deborah Ellis

7. What precautions did they establish when they started their secret school?

_____

_____

8. How do you think Nooria was able to find someone to marry in these difficult circumstances?

_____

_____

Language Activities:

1. Reassemble the word parts listed below into eight compound words found in this chapter.

room	care	shine	work	home	some	any	one
class	market	times	place	sun	ful	body	every

a) _____   b) _____

c) _____   d) _____

e) _____   f) _____

g) _____   h) _____

2. This chapter ends with the statements: "You'll never guess,' her mother said. 'Nooria's getting married." Here is another example of a **cliffhanger**. How else might the author have revealed that the Nooria was getting married, in a cliffhanger sort of way.

_____

_____

_____

_____

The Breadwinner
By Deborah Ellis

Chapter 13

Before you read the chapter:

Parvana begins the chapter by telling her sister, Nooria, "But you've never even met him!" Think of one advantage and one disadvantage to an "arranged marriage" such as this one.

Advantage: _____

_____

Disadvantage: _____

_____

Think of three qualities you consider it important for a person to find in a marriage partner.

_____

_____

_____

Vocabulary:

Think of **synonyms** for the following words. Try to think of at least two per word. Use a thesaurus if necessary.

fetch: _____

seldom: _____

inform: _____

satisfaction: _____

squirmed: _____

insist: _____

responsible: _____

accompany: _____

The Breadwinner
By Deborah Ellis

Questions:

Complete the following summary of Chapter 13, filling in the appropriate words from the box in each of the spaces.

Taliban	burqa	empty	crying	October	building	truck
neighbor	school	pen	Mazar-e-Sharif	pocket	Mrs. Weera	

The person that Nooria planned to marry had been their _____ for many years. Nooria planned to move to the town of _____ where the Taliban were not in control. There she would be able to go to _____. Nooria and her mother would be away until the month of _____. _____ would look after Parvana while they were gone. Nooria and her mother would be traveling in the back of a _____. Nooria said that as soon as she got out of Taliban territory, she would throw off her _____ and tear it into a million pieces. As a going away present, Parvana bought her sister a _____. With her mother and the others gone, the apartment seemed _____. Mrs. Weera insisted that Parvana keep some of her wages for _____ money. One day Parvana was caught inside an old bombed-out _____ during a storm. There she heard the sound of someone _____.

Language Activities:

Parvana's mother tells her daughter "you think you're above yourself". What does this expression mean? Can you think of two additional expressions that are commonly used, but people of another culture might not understand?

_____

_____

_____

_____

The Breadwinner
By Deborah Ellis

Chapter 14

Before you read the chapter:

Chapter 14 introduces us to a character who endured tremendous emotional suffering in her life, and is now having difficulty going on. If you were Parvana and Mrs. Weera, how would you go about nursing this person back to health. After you read the chapter, go back and check your answer to see if your strategy was similar to that of the characters' in the novel.

_____

_____

_____

Vocabulary:

Draw a straight line to connect the vocabulary word to its definition. Remember to use a straight edge (like a ruler).

1.	rummage	a)	proof
2.	curfew	b)	pause
3.	grope	c)	important
4.	browse	d)	to hunt or ransack
5.	progress	e)	hallway
6.	corridor	f)	fumble
7.	hesitate	g)	make headway
8.	critical	h)	to scan or thumb over
9.	evidence	i)	poke
10.	prod	j)	bedtime

The Breadwinner

By Deborah Ellis

Questions:

1. Why do you think Parvana told the strange woman in the bombed-out building her secret?

   _____

   _____

2. Why did the fact that the woman did not have a burqa upset Parvana?

   _____

3. What was Parvana's strategy in getting the woman safely to her apartment?

   _____

   _____

4. Who did Parvana pretend to be during this adventure? Why do you think she found it necessary to pretend?

   _____

   _____

5. Describe the welcome that Mrs. Weera gave to the woman.

   _____

   _____

6. a) Why was the news that Homa brought so distressing to Parvana?

   _____

   b) What was Parvana's immediate response to this bad piece of news?

   _____

   _____

   c) What was it that finally convinced her to return to the market?

   _____

   _____

The Breadwinner
By Deborah Ellis

Language Activities:

1. Beside each pair of words write **A** (antonym) or **S** (synonym) or **H** (homonym).

   a) so – sew _____   **f)** hair – hare _____

   b) tightly – loosely _____   **g)** carry – tote _____

   c) allowed – aloud _____   **h)** dyed – died _____

   d) first – last _____   **i)** important – trivial _____

   e) want – desire _____   **j)** sun – son _____

2. Homa experiences terror and heartache like few people do. In your own words, describe what the word terror means to you.

   _____

   _____

   _____

   _____

   How is terror different then fear?

   _____

   _____

Extension Activities:

You have been given the task of creating a poster for a local Book Fair. Design a poster with the purpose of getting other students to read *The Breadwinner*. Your poster should include the novel's title, author, an attractive picture, and a very brief description of what the novel is about. You might want to check out the design of other book posters in the school library before beginning this project.

The Breadwinner

By Deborah Ellis

Chapter 15

Before you read the chapter:

Of all the characters you have met in *The Breadwinner,* which have you find the most interesting? Explain your choice.

_____

_____

How would you describe Parvana's personality? Think of at least three character traits that best describe her.

_____

_____

Vocabulary:

Choose a word from the list that means the same or nearly the same as the underlined word(s).

karachi	broth	poultice	derision
refugees	transport	exiled	confident

1. Parvana placed all of her belongings on the **cart**.   _____

2. Mrs. Weera made **soup** for the sick woman.   _____

3. The doctor applied a **dressing** to the soldier's wound.   _____

4. The president was treated with **great disrespect**.   _____

5. The camp was for **displaced people**.   _____

6. I will **send** the machine part to you immediately.   _____

7. The king was **sent out of the country**.   _____

8. The actor was very **self-assured**.   _____

The Breadwinner
By Deborah Ellis

Questions:

1. Explain how Parvana's father came home from prison.

   _____

   _____

2. What did Parvana do to help her father recover (at least two things)?

   _____

   _____

3. Why do you think having her father back filled Parvana with hope?

   _____

   _____

4. What additional motivation did Shauzia now have to leave home?

   _____

   _____

5. When Parvana asks her father if he is well enough to travel he says, "I will never be well enough". What do you think he meant by this statement?

   _____

   _____

6. What explanation did Parvana's father give for his release from prison?

   _____

   _____

7. Why do you think it was important to Parvana that she plant the flowers where the window woman could see them?

   _____

   _____

8. What did Parvana and Shauzia agree to do in 20 years? What did you think about this promise?

   _____

   _____

The Breadwinner

By Deborah Ellis

Language Activities:

1. Create a time line for *The Breadwinner* indicating the ten most important events of the novel and the order in which they happened.

2. The conclusion of *The Breadwinner* presents another **cliffhanger** – the perfect invitation for an exciting sequel to be written continuing Parvana's adventures. Deborah Ellis, in fact, has written a sequel to this novel entitled *Parvana's Journey*. In a paragraph or two describe what you think will happen to Parvana and her family in the sequel to *The Breadwinner*.

    _____

    _____

    _____

    _____

    _____

    _____

    _____

    _____

    _____

Answer Key

Chapter 1: *(page 10)*

Vocabulary:

1. **a)** 2   **b)** 4   **c)** 5   **d)** 1   **e)** 3
2. **a)** disrupt   **b)** hawked   **c)** peddler   **d)** urn   **e)** labyrinth
   f) militia   **g)** definite   **h)** collapse   **i)** decreed   **j)** respected
3. Answers may vary.

Questions:

1. They couldn't go outside or attend school.
2. Answers may vary. (e.g., she was small, tended to be outspoken, afraid of the Taliban)
3. **a)** By selling things in the marketplace and by reading and writing for people.
   b) He had been a high school teacher.
4. Answers may vary. (e.g., women should not be in public places; against education)
5. They sold tea to customers who couldn't leave their own shops.
6. Answers may vary.
7. Her parents could no longer teach for a living, and each home they moved to was destroyed by bombs.
8. **a)** She said that Parvana was such an ugly baby the Soviets couldn't stand to be in the same country with her.
   b) Nooria had a sharp tongue.

Language Activities:

1. **a)** was in grade six   **b)** five years old   **c)** two years old   **d)** the oldest sister
2. Answers may vary. (e.g., Perhaps Parvana will consider other jobs she might do to support her family, including being a "tea boy".)

Chapter 2: *(page 14)*

Vocabulary:

1. *toshak* – a narrow mattress   *shalwar kameez* – long, loose shirt and trousers
   Eid – a Moslem festival   *nan* – flat Afghan bread
   turban – head covering
2. Crossword Puzzle

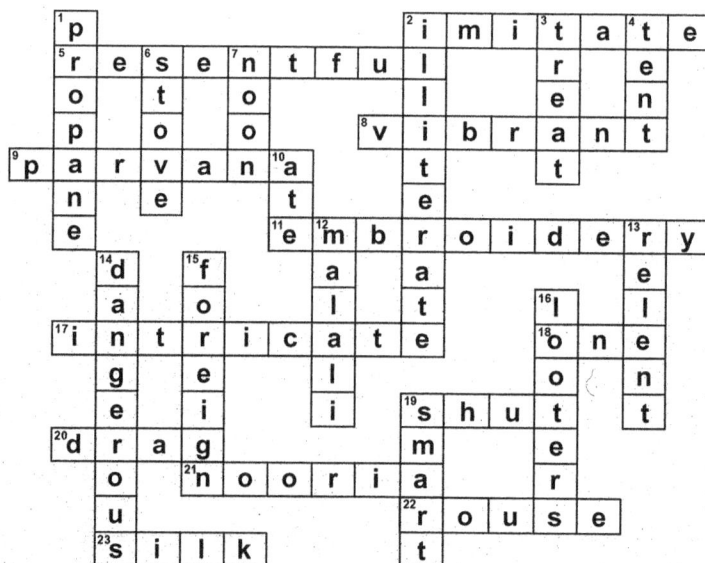

Questions:

1. They could be arrested or beaten by the Taliban.
2. boredom, something to do

3. Answers may vary. (e.g., complaints, rebellious talk)
4. Nooria would be married in them.
5. Answers may vary.
6. He was killed by a land mine.
7. Sitting around a plastic cloth spread out over the floor.
8. She led the Afghan troops in a victorious charge against the British just when the battle seemed lost.
9. Answers may vary. (e.g., Not all battles are fought by soldiers on the battlefield, some are fought by courageous people who take a stand against what is wrong.)
10. They felt Parvana's father was promoting foreign ideas and suspected that he posessed forbidden literature.

Language Activities:
Answers may vary.

Chapter 3: *(page 18)*
Vocabulary:
1. agree – the other words all mean protest
2. celebration – the other words all have to do with laws
3. laboratory – the other words all mean the bathroom
4. devotion – the other words all mean being able to tell something apart
5. affluent – the other words all mean performing an act
6. pranced – the other words all mean to stumble or move haltingly
7. drillers – the other words all are associated with the military.

Questions:

After waking up following her father's arrest, Parvana and her family decided to clean up their **apartment**. The family slept on quilts and blankets spread over the **floor**. In the past, whenever Parvana awaken in the night, the sound of her father's **snoring** made her think that everything was alright.

Parvana's mother had often said, "You can't be truly Afghan if you don't know someone who's been in **prison**".

The Talaban had ordered that all windows be painted black so that no one could see the **women** inside.

Parvana's mother decided that she and **Parvana** would get her husband out of jail. Nooria wrote her a note which pretended to be from their **father** giving Parvana's mother permission to be outside by herself. The billowing **burqa** Parvana's mother was wearing made it hard for her to see where she was going. Along the way they used a **photograph** to ask people if they had seen Parvana's father. At the prison Parvana and her mother told the **guards** that they wanted to see Parvana's father. To give her strength, Parvana imagined she was the Afghan heroine, **Malali**. Parvana and her mother finally gave up and left the prison after the guards began to **beat** them.

Language Activities:
1. Answers may vary.
2. Answers may vary. (e.g., cup/board)

Chapter 4: *(page 21)*
Vocabulary:
1. i)   2. g)   3. h)   4. d)   5. c)   6. j)   7. a)   8. e)   9. f)   10. b)

Questions:
1. a year and a half
2. **a)** There was no one to read it or publish it.
   b) As educated people it was their responsibility to rebuild their country.
3. **a)** He wanted to stay to be a part of rebuilding the country.
   b) Answers may vary.

4. They all lived in one small room.
5. a) They must rely on each other to survive their ordeal.
   b) Nooria had a tendency to be negative / selfish.
6. Her mother was the parent and had always assumed the authority in the family.
7. a) She was suffering from depression.
   b) Answers will vary. (e.g., Too many stressful things happened to her and her family and it just became too much for her to bear.)
8. She knew there was no other way for them to survive. It was also the most logical solution to their problem – Parvana was more familiar now with the outside world.

Language Activities:
1. Answers will vary.
2. sandals, burqas, feet, families, wives, parents, countries, tongues, pieces, persons or people

Chapter 5: *(page 25)*
Vocabulary:
1. selections	2. attendant	3. anxious	4. circumstance
5. sensible	6. warily	7. fetch	8. an eternity
9. consider	10. obedient		

Questions:
1. Men were supposed to do all the shopping; a woman couldn't go into the shops.
2. Answers may vary. (e.g., She was still young and might be able to get away with it.)
3. A Talib began to beat her for being in the marketplace without her father.
4. Answers may vary. (e.g., She was outgoing, bossy, encouraging.)
5. Through her encouragement and leadership she got Parvana's mother back on her feet.
6. Without her mother providing leadership, this responsibility had fallen to Nooria.
7. It was contaminated and would make a person sick to drink it.
8. Answers may vary. (Perhaps students will begin to link this with what the title of the book might mean.)
9. She had someone to share the leadership with.

Language Activities:
1. Answers may vary.
2. magazine, selection, servants, shopkeepers, shoulder, smell, squeezing, stick, suddenly, swallowed

Chapter 6: *(page 28)*
Vocabulary: Word Search
Questions:
1. Answers may vary.

2. Because of their isolation, they no close friends who would question this.
3. a) Parvana: she had to have her hair cut; dress differently; take on a dangerous responsibility.
   b) Her mother: Parvana was now wearing Hossain's clothes which brought back painful memories.
4. Answers may vary. (e.g., having long hair no longer seemed important)
5. If she was caught being dressed as a boy by the Taliban she would be punished.
6. In case someone came to the house unexpectedly, their secret wouldn't be found out.
7. Answers may vary. (e.g., She was frustrated and unhappy with her situation.)
8. a) Parvana's mother called Ali by his dead brother Hossain's name.
   b) Answers may vary. (e.g., Perhaps she was half asleep and dreaming.)

Language Activities:
1. a) **P**arvana's brother**,** **H**ossain**,** was killed by a land mine**.**
   b) **T**he **Af**ghan city of **K**abul was seriously damaged by years of war**.**
   c) **W**hat kind of president would it take to restore order in **Af**ghanistan**?**
2. Answers may vary.

Chapter 7: *(page 31)*
Vocabulary:
Answers may vary.

Questions:
1. She got outside of the house for a change and didn't have to do housework.
2. People got used to seeing her there and would seek her out if they wanted to hire her to read or write.
3. Answers may vary. (e.g., It was very dangerous; being a girl made her very vulnerable in that situation.)
4. Read a letter.
5. Answers may vary. (e.g., a) Niece: she was getting married and moving to Afghanistan. Her father was a good man. b) Aunt: she lived in Germany; she was a caring person who loved her family.)
6. Answers may vary. (e.g., He loved his wife. He was a caring man with feelings.)
7. Answers may vary. (e.g., Advantage: avoided the hassle of haggling; might get more than they bargained for; might not anger the Talib. Disadvantage: might get much less for their job.)
8. Answers may vary. (e.g., Advantage: if you were good at bartering, then you would do very well. Disadvantage: if you were not very good at it, then you would not do well.)

Language Activities:
1. Answers may vary.
2. Answers may vary. (e.g. *Person against Person* – Taliban against Parvana's family; family members squabbling in the small house. *Person against Nature* – polluted drinking water; hot, uncomfortable climate. *Person against self* – Parvana's mother especially struggles to maintain her spirits during the trials faced by her family.

Chapter 8: *(page 35)*
Vocabulary:
1. routine 2. position 3. dawdling 4. distinctive 5. pneumonia
6. splendid 7. athletics 8. relent 9. escort 10. collided

Questions:
1. F 2. T 3. T 4. F 5. F 6. F 7. T 8. T 9. F 10. F

Language Activities:
Answers may vary.

Chapter 9: *(page 37)*

Vocabulary:

1. a) **2.** c) **3.** a) **4.** b) **5.** d) **6.** c) **7.** a) **8.** b)

Questions:

1. She met a former classmate, Shauzia, who was a "tea boy" in the marketplace.
2. dried apricots
3. Her father died and her brother went to find work in Iran. That would mean there was no adult male in their family to earn a living.
4. They are never heard from again.
5. Answers may vary.
6. She didn't want to stay long.
7. They would make more money. They could move with the crowd.
8. Starting a school for the children and publishing a magazine for Afghani women.
9. Nooria would teach in the school.
10. She was a woman who lived in the apartment near Parvana's spot in the marketplace. She would throw little items that she had made from her window down to Parvana.
11. Answers may vary.

Language Activities:

1. Answers may vary.
2. watch, dress, care, boss, excite, sweet, hear, invite

Chapter 10: *(page 41)*

Vocabulary:

obedient – defiant   intact – apart   stingy – generous
accommodate – turn away   recognize – forget

1. accommodate **2.** intact **3.** recognize **4.** obedient **5.** stingy

Questions:

1. **a)** bone-digging   **b)** Answers may vary.
2. He sold them to someone else.
3. a skull
4. She had to go to the bathroom, but there was no latrine nearby.
5. **a)** to kill children   **b)** Answers may vary.
6. three days
7. **a)** to save money for their trays   **b)** Answers may vary.
8. to wash away the images of what she had done all day

Language Activities:

1. Answers may vary. (e.g., Nouns: sky, clouds, bones; Verbs: destroyed, sells, pecked; Adjectives: large, gray, generous)
2. Answers may vary.

Chapter 11: *(page 44)*

Vocabulary:

1. firmly **2.** calm **3.** terrified **4.** declared **5.** relent
6. disrespect **7.** ordinary **8.** intimidate **9.** escort **10.** stint

Questions:

1. She probably needed to tell someone about what she had been through that day.
2. chicken feed, cooking oil, soap and buttons
3. Parvana was normally very obedient and compliant to her mother's wishes, so this was very unusual.
4. Answers may vary.

5. a) Answers may vary. (i.e., Although it was very unpleasant work, Parvana did what was necessary in order for her family to survive.)
   b) Answers may vary.
6. The weight of the items.
7. She had gained respect for Parvana.
8. They witnessed thieves having their hands chopped off.

Language Activities:
Answers may vary.

Chapter 12: *(page 47)*
Vocabulary:
1. enthusiastic   2. preferred   3. depend   4. nomads   5. insisted
6. fertile   7. snippet   8. ceased   9. incident   10. tempted

Questions:
1. She had been shaken up by what she had witnessed in the stadium.
2. Answers may vary. (e.g., western influence – trivial)
3. a) She liked the pictures she had seen of France and its people.
   b) She would have to find a way out of the country and all the way to France, which was far away.
4. Answers will vary. (e.g., will require a lot of planning and help from adults)
5. a princess
6. Answers may vary. (e.g., perhaps sell her products in the marketplace)
7. two groups; never at the same time two days in a row
8. Answers may vary. (e.g., someone she knew from the past)

Language Activities:
1. a) sunshine   b) sometimes   c) everyone   d) anybody   e) classroom
   f) homework   g) marketplace   h) careful
2. Answers may vary.

Chapter 13: *(page 50)*
Vocabulary:
Answers may vary.

Questions:
   The person that Nooria planned to marry had been their **neighbor** for many years. Nooria planned to move to the town of **Mazar-e-Sharif** where the **Taliban** were not in control. There she would be able to go to **school**. Nooria and her mother would be away until the month of **October**. **Mrs. Weera** would look after Parvana while they were gone. Nooria and her mother would be traveling in the back of a **truck**. Nooria said that as soon as she got out of Taliban territory, she would throw off her **burqa** and tear it into a million pieces. As a going away present, Parvana bought her sister a **pen**.
   With her mother and the others gone, the apartment seemed almost **empty**. Mrs. Weera insisted that Parvana keep some of her wages for **pocket** money.
   One day Parvana was caught inside an old bombed-out **building** during a storm. There she heard the sound of someone **crying**.

Language Activities:
Answers may vary.

Chapter 14: *(page 52)*

Vocabulary:

1. d)   2. j)   3. f)   4. h)   5. g)   6. e)   7. b)   8. c)   9. a)   10. i)

Questions:

1. Answers may vary. (e.g., perhaps nervousness; or to encourage her to talk)
2. Parvana knew the woman was in danger without one.
3. To wait until it was dark and keep out of sight as much as possible.
4. Malali. Answers may vary. (e.g., to keep her mind occupied)
5. She didn't hesitate to give the woman a warm welcome.
6. **a)** The Taliban had captured the city that Parvana's mother and sister had gone to.
   b) disbelief, then she stayed on the toshak for two days
   c) Shauzia's prodding.

Language Activities:

1. **a)** H   **b)** A   **c)** H   **d)** A   **e)** S   **f)** H   **g)** S   **h)** H   **i)** A   **j)** H
2. Answers may vary.

Chapter 15: *(page 55)*

Vocabulary:

1. karachi   2. broth   3. poultice   4. derision   5. refugees
6. transport   7. exiled   8. confident

Questions:

1. A couple of men brought him home from the prison.
2. Answers may vary. (e.g., by getting water from the tap; by keeping Mrs. Weera's granddaughter quiet so he could rest)
3. Answers may vary.
4. Her grandfather had started to look for a husband for Shauzia.
5. He knew he would never completely recover his health.
6. "I don't know why they arrested me. How would I know why they let me go?"
7. Answers may vary. (e.g., perhaps to give the woman hope and thank her for the gifts)
8. To meet at the top of the Eiffel Tower in Paris. Answers may vary.

Language Activities:

1. Answers may vary.
2. Answers may vary.